FINDING AND GROWING YOUR FIELD

FINDING AND GROWING YOUR FIELD

A Guide for Rookie Football Coaches

Transitioning from High School to College Division 1

Copyright © 2023 by Jabbar Juluke

All rights reserved.

No portion of this book may be reproduced in any form without written permission from the publisher or author, except as permitted by U.S. copyright law.

1st Edition

Printed in the United States of America

FINDING AND GROWING YOUR FIELD

A Guide for Rookie Football Coaches
Transitioning from High School to College Division 1

JABBAR JULUKE

Eight Ambitions / The Eight Eighteen LLC
New Orleans

In loving memory

Byron Honoré Sr.

December 15, 1957 – December 22, 2022

To my beloved brother, though you may no longer walk beside me in this earthly journey, your presence remains etched in the deepest corners of my heart. Your laughter, your wisdom, and your unwavering support are the guiding stars that illuminate my path. In your honor, I dedicate these words, a testament to the profound impact you've had on my life and the lives of all who were fortunate enough to know you. Though we may be separated by time and space, the bond we shared transcends the boundaries of mortality. You are forever cherished, forever missed, and forever loved. Rest in peace, dear brother.

Table of Contents

Foreword — 1

Introduction — 5

PART 1: HIGH SCHOOL GROWTH — 15

CHAPTER 1: As the Head Coach of a Position — 17

CHAPTER 2: As a Coordinator — 21

CHAPTER 3: As a Head Coach in High School — 29

CHAPTER 4: Building Team Trust — 43

CHAPTER 5: Building Relationships with College Coaches — 47

PART 2: COLLEGE GROWTH — 51

CHAPTER 6: How to Prepare for College Coaching Interviews — 53

CHAPTER 7: As a College Coach — 59

CHAPTER 8: What To Look For When Recruiting — 63

CHAPTER 9: Mentorship — 69

CHAPTER 10: Networking — 73

CHAPTER 11: Finding the Right Partner — 75

Quick Do's and Don'ts for Coaches — 79

About the Author — 81

Foreword by
John Hiser

When Jabbar asked me to write the foreword to his book, I was, of course, honored to be asked, especially considering the vast number of friends, relatives, colleagues, and contacts that he has accumulated over the course of his lifetime. One thing that I have understood about coaching is that coaches seem to have the largest network in the western world! If you truly need to get information, ask the right coach; chances are that you will get it soon, straightforwardly, and worth your time.

I was the principal of Edna Karr Junior High School, Edna Karr Magnet School, and Edna Karr High School from 1985 until 2013. Since its founding, our school has had a very strong reputation for both academics and activities. We have had extremely successful subject matter specialists in the classroom and highly successful coaches and sponsors outside of it. The Karr junior football program began in 1964, with Johnny Owens as its first head coach, and when he retired in 1980, Don

Wattigny took over. After a few years, Al Ott became the head coach, and in 1990, the Orleans Parish School Board voted for Karr to become a 7-12 magnet school. In 1991, we hired Don Wattigny to return to become our first head coach of the new high school football team. Don remained in the position until he retired in 2002.

So, in the winter of 2002-03, we advertised for a new head coach. Sometime in February or March, our interview committee met to make the selection. Strangely, we only had five applicants. I knew some but not others. The candidate I was leaning toward notified us that he had withdrawn his application, and I really was at a loss as we began our interviews.

In every interview, I believed that the committee person who makes the final decision has a "The Question" question. Mine was "Coach, how will you know that your program is successful?" Each of the first four candidates answered by raising his fist in a fist punch and said something to the effect of, "When we can wear the ring!" Then the fifth candidate came in. He seemed articulate, respectful, young, and bright. To each of the prior questions, he answered in a similar way to the others, yet more upbeat and in a much more concise manner. And then came my question at the end.

Jabbar's answer was, "Mr. Hiser, I won't feel successful until I see my boys walking into church with their wives and children; when I see them walking down the street holding their son's hand, and when I see them walking into the voting booth with their daughters to cast their votes. I seek to build more than football players; I seek to build good citizens, good men." His answer indicated to me a value system that was a vital ingredient toward teaching the whole student-athlete. Suffice it to say, I was sold, and so was the committee. Jabbar remained the Edna Karr head coach through the 2012-13 season and left for LA Tech at that point.

During that time, Karr made the playoffs each year and played in the state championship game three times in a row, winning in 2012, his last season with us. While Jabbar was head coach at Karr, he and I had some disagreements over stuff, but it was always about just stuff; I never questioned his commitment or his character. Another facet of his style was that it was seldom if ever "his" team; it was almost always "our" team. His goal was not just football; his focus was about the program, both athletics, academics as well as other activities. He understood that when the team played, over 300 students performed; the program was much bigger than the team. I never had to remind him of that because his vision was expansive, not exclusive.

His program's success may in part be due to his record and the state championship. However, his legacy is in his players. They are college grads, teachers, coaches (recreational, high school, and college levels), entrepreneurs, and the like. As he said during the interview, "I'll know if my program is successful when I see what they are doing ten years after they leave the program." By any definition, Jabbar's tenure was successful.

Introduction

My Journey from Junior High to College Coaching

You're not good enough for the NFL.

This breaking realization came to me in 1995 as I was nearing the end of my college football career. My only option was to find something that would connect me to the sport I had dedicated my life to. Eventually, coaching became my saving grace.

My brother-in-law Lionel Roberts, who was the head coach of my former stomping grounds Phillips Junior High at the time, offered me an opportunity to join him in coaching. While it was only a team of middle schoolers, I fell in love with the job. Being on *this* side of the game both intrigued and fulfilled me in ways I never imagined possible. I established a track record of success in my first year and was determined to advance to high school coaching.

When I got word that Al Jones was looking for a few coaches to join him at Douglass High School in town, I took a chance and called him. Soon after introducing myself, things began to work in my favor.

INTRODUCTION

"Man, I recognize your name," he said.

As it turns out, Al Jones played for the same team as my brother, Byron Honore, from 1972 to 1974. That alone landed me the job on the spot.

"You're hired!" he blurted out, having never seen me before.

At 7:30 the next morning, I was standing on the high school football field with a clipboard in hand.

The job also demanded that I become a substitute teacher at the school, which soon gave me a rude awakening. The students were so disrespectful that I questioned *everything*. What kept me was my love for coaching; I had to eventually accept the fact that this experience came with the position.

I had nothing at the time. I had not finished college at Southern University at New Orleans (SUNO) yet. I did not own a car and was living with my mother. My Aunt Junita Juluke worked as a Title I Coordinator at Douglass and kindly offered to drive me to work every day. Towards the end of spring 1997, she said, "Okay, now what are we going to do? You can't be a substitute teacher for the rest of your life." I felt comfortable in my coaching job even if I did have to substitute from time to time, but Aunt Juanita saw bigger plans for me. "No, you need to go back to school," she said. That summer, with a Pell Grant and student loans, I was back in college, continuing my education, and making my Aunt Juanita proud. In the fall of that same year, she would continue to drop me off to college every morning—and I would catch the bus from

Southern to Douglas to work for the rest of the afternoon. Everything was lining up for me.

Following my stint at Douglas, I found myself at Brother Martin High School, where I recruited some recognizable names: D.J. Augustine, Courtley Wallace, Corey Bloom, and Ryan Brock. I was taking my first steps toward becoming a true team advocate. My search for a greater challenge led me to Anthony Biagas, my former high school coach at St. Augustine. I did not find that challenge on the football field, unfortunately.

They did not let me coach, I was essentially an overpaid water boy. I knew I did not want to spend the rest of my career at Saint Augustine, so in school I worked toward getting into the post-baccalaureate education program and becoming a certified teacher. I balanced all of this while showing up to hydrate the St. Augustine football team. After two years there, I heard that an old high school friend, Frank Wilson, was looking for two coaches, and I jumped at the chance. When we met about the position, I could sense Frank's passion and determination, which was something I lacked at St. Augustine.

When I arrived for my interview with Coach Wilson on a Friday afternoon, it was clear that he was ready for me to commit right away. That upcoming Monday was my birthday, so I offered to begin coaching on Tuesday.

"We still practice on Monday, and you need to be here," he said.

"It's my birthday!" I responded.

INTRODUCTION

"And? You need to get your ass here to work," he said. So, just like that, on Monday, my birthday was celebrated on the football field.

There was a time I was planning to close on my first house. When I mentioned to Coach Frank that the date was falling on the same day as an upcoming game, and that I'd be a little late. He said, "man listen, I'm happy for you because it's an opportunity of a lifetime to buy your first house, but you can not miss the game. Or be late for the game." When the day arrived, I rushed my way to the Behrman Stadium in record time, to make it there before the game started. If Coach Frank taught me anything, it was *dedication*. In my eighth year as a coach, we went to the State Championship with sixteen Division 1 football players on that St. Augustine team. Dayrl Johnson, Milton Collins, Cedric Henry, Busta Davis, Kennan Lewis, and Mike Wallace—all would go on to the NFL.

During this time, I was still in the process of completing my certification to become a teacher, so moving up in coaching wasn't at the forefront of my mind. But, one day, while reading the local newspaper, that all changed. My eyes were drawn to the story of Coach Don Wattigny's resignation as Karr's head coach. The article announced that the team was extending the deadline for interested coaches. Before I applied, I asked Coach Frank about it.

"What do you think about me applying for the Karr job?"

"Yeah, I think you should do it," he said.

His agreement was all I needed. I was filled with ambition and confidence until the night before the interview. I suddenly got cold feet. I pondered on the thought that they were not going to hire me and that I was wasting my time. In need of some encouragement, I called a good friend, Daryn White, who did his best to push me to go to the interview anyway. Still not convinced, called up my brother, Clarence Paris, and told him the same thing. "I'm picking your ass up," he said. "You gotta go!"

When I arrived at the Holiday Inn, the Athletic Director, Roch Weilbaecher (who was also my childhood AAU basketball coach) greeted me in the lobby. He told me I had a good chance at becoming head coach and encouraged me to put my best foot forward. When he told me that, I just relaxed. Okay, I think I've got a chance. I thought.

With my head held high, I walked into the interview meeting room with a panel of seven people. They inquired about my philosophies. The most important question was, "Where do you see the program in fifteen years?"

"I hope that you guys don't judge me off the wins and losses on a football field. We will win some games, and we're going to lose some games." I explained. "Don't get me wrong, I'm a winner. I want to win, but I really want you guys to judge me off of my first graduating class, 2003- 2004. I want you to judge me on the graduation success rate from high school ten years from now and whether or not they graduated from college. If they have a family now, or if they are married. I want you to judge me on how many productive citizens in society that I have helped to mold. That's the win-loss record that I wish you all would judge me on."

INTRODUCTION

With that answer, I was hired. Twenty-nine years old with no experience as a head coach, and I was in! The rest was history. Every year of my career as head coach at Karr, we went to the playoffs.

Things took a turn for the better after we hauled through the tribulations of Hurricane Katrina. It was 2005 and my third year at Karr. Because of Katrina, we didn't even get a chance at a season! But we still managed to clinch the 2012 championship!"

That's when people started to discuss the good chances of me moving up to the college level.

"You're going to college! You can coach in college!" Those were the resounding words of people at my church and neighborhood. Despite their support, it was difficult for me to wrap my head around the idea of leaving the program that I had built. My dream was to be the best coach in the state of Louisiana, but it didn't have to be at the collegiate level. I would always tell my staff that the goal was to build a dynamic, successful high school program.

As a program, we engaged in a comprehensive study, drawing inspiration from esteemed counterparts like John Curtis, West Monroe, Neville, and St. Augustine. Our primary objective revolved around emulating their enduring success while preserving our dominance over an extended period. Brice Brown and I frequently convened to envision the future of our program, ensuring that our young men had the opportunity to pursue higher education and excel in football at the highest echelons. To realize this vision, we acknowledged the imperative for heightened discipline, superior physical conditioning, and a profound understanding of our adversaries.

In our quest to unravel the secrets of these triumphant programs, Brice and I made it a point to attend state championship games. While I attended openly, positioned at the highest vantage point within the stadium, I keenly observed as the teams made their grand entrances. This experience provided invaluable insights into the ideals to which our team should aspire if we wished to join the esteemed ranks of Louisiana's football greats.

During those days, I meticulously scrutinized and documented their conduct: their pre-game rituals, team dynamics, and the cohesive synergy among the coaching staff. These observations served as a blueprint for us to effect changes and elevate our own program. However, our mission extended beyond the confines of the football field; our commitment equally lay in molding our young men into exemplary citizens, future husbands, and responsible fathers. Above all else, this noble aspiration remained our paramount goal.

We didn't want to be one-hit wonders; we wanted our high school, players, and performance to be talked about for years to come. That was the height of my dream. But, Doug Blackman, another coach at Karr, helped me change my perspective. "You need to strike while the iron is hot," he said. "This is my fortieth year coaching, and I never tried. You can always come back. Go try!"

During this run to the State Championship, I was doing interviews with any and everybody to give the school as much publicity as we

INTRODUCTION

possibly could. I wanted the kids to get some notoriety and get an opportunity to play college football. A guy named Todd Black with ESPN Radio, who had interviewed me three times over the phone, sent me a text after we won. Would you be interested in coaching at Louisiana Tech? When I showed the text to my wife, Denise, she yelled out, "Yeah, you're interested!" I wasn't going to argue with her, so I texted him yes.

The Monday after the State Championship, Coach Holtz from Louisiana Tech called to personally ask if I'd be interested in coaching on his staff. (First, I thought it was a prank phone call. I mean, I couldn't believe that I was actually speaking with him directly.) He went on to explain that he talked to twenty different coaches and twenty different people in Louisiana. He told them that he wanted to hire a minority high school coach from our state. "Everyone that I talked to gave me five or six different names," he said. "But all twenty of them gave me your name. Can you be here at eight o'clock tomorrow morning?"

I agreed and went to call my wife immediately. "We need a hotel room in North Louisiana," I told her. "Don't ask any questions. I can explain it to you on the way up."

The next morning, I sat before Coach Skip Holtz and David Gibbs. I went into the meeting thinking I'd be taking on the defensive backs coaching position because that is what I played. But they had other plans for me. Kenneth Dixon and Tevin King were returning as running backs for their sophomore year, and the coaches could see they needed a mentor on and off the field. My outlook on promoting players for success convinced them that I was the guy for the job, so I became the Louisiana Tech running back coach.

FINDING AND GROWING YOUR FIELDS

That day marked the beginning of an eleven-year career in coaching college football. I spent the next three years at Louisiana Tech, and I will always have love for Coach Holtz for giving me my first opportunity to coach college football. *How Bout them Dogs!*

From there, I spent one month at Texas Tech with Coach Kliff Kingsbury, but then, I left there to go back to my home state to LSU. Coach Kingsbury was extremely supportive of this move. He was a great coach and an even better man. I was at LSU for a year with Coach Les Miles and learned so much in my short time with him. LSU is a very special place, and I loved every moment I was there. Geaux Tigers!

Eventually, I made my way back to Texas Tech. The Texas Tech community embraced my wife and I with open arms. During this time, we were battling cancer and she had to go through chemotherapy. We had the best care from UMC of Lubbock. We are forever grateful to our Texas Tech family. Guns Up!

Now, I am back in my home state at the University of Louisiana with Coach Billy Napier! *Geaux Cajuns*!

Currently we are at the University of Florida and we are headed into our 3rd season! The University of Florida has embraced my family and I with open arms. I am very fortunate to say I am the Running Backs Coach at the University of Florida. It is an honor and I am looking forward to doing great things! *Go Gators!*

I am writing this book with a heartfelt purpose: to inspire young high school coaches through my extraordinary journey. My aim is to illuminate the arduous path I had to navigate in order to ascend to the next level. It

13

INTRODUCTION

was not a smooth road, but it was one paved with unwavering perseverance. This is my passion, and my goal is to touch as many lives as I possibly can. My story carries the potential to encourage countless young individuals. Sports, particularly football, serves as a powerful equalizer in life. The lessons we learn on the field can be seamlessly applied to real-life situations, helping us navigate the highs and lows of our journey. If this book can leave an impact on one person or a multitude, I will be elated to have shared my life's story with the world. Football saved my life, and I shudder to think where I would be without it. We need coaches, both men and women, to continue shaping the future of our youth. Through this book, I pray to inspire the next generation of coaches to guide our young people in the right direction, instilling values of respect for one another and for those who have paved the way.

Two scriptures from the Bible resonate deeply with me: Luke 12:48, "To whom much is given; much is required," and John 13:7, where JESUS replied, 'You don't understand now what I'm doing, but someday you will.' I wholeheartedly embrace this assignment – to save as many lives as I can by being the best possible role model and mentor."

When I embarked on this journey, I had no idea where it would lead me. I'm grateful that I chose to fall in love with football and the opportunity to influence the lives of our youth. This industry is in dire need of positive role models, both on and off the field. We hold a unique position to inspire, guide, and educate, and it's our responsibility to prepare and empower our young athletes. If you're reading this book, go mold our youth!

Part 1

HIGH SCHOOL GROWTH

Chapter 1

As the Head Coach of a Position

There will always be a new goal, a better job, or a new team to look forward to. However, it is critical to recognize that being present in your current role supports each of your career steps ahead. You will thrive if you plant yourself where you are and operate from a *position* of excellence.

Staying Loyal

To different people, loyalty means different things. Aligning your professional presentation and decisions with the head coach's can make or break your chances. Make sure you are always dressed appropriately because you are a reflection of your head coach. Remember, he hired you because he believed in you. Conducting yourself in a way that your head coach likes, accepts, and appreciates is a sign of not only loyalty but also respect. Another form of loyalty is ensuring that you are prepared for daily activities with your players and the team. Check that your practice script and individual drills are well-organized.

Finally, listen to your head coach. Learning the philosophy of the head coach is vital because you are an extension of him. The head coach is making decisions that affect the entire team, he must be able to trust you to convey the same message to our position group and players.

Many assistants, including myself, have discussed what they would have done differently than the head coach in certain situations. This lack of backing will lead to division and distrust. So, be the extension and help to build the program rather than demolish it. This was not always my way of thinking. I wanted to push the program further when I was a young, eager coach at Douglass High School. I thought my way was the only way, but I went about it incorrectly. I wasn't behaving in the way that I believe a man should. Instead of trying to get Coach Al Jones to understand what I was trying to bring to the team and give him my ideas on how we could improve, I was complaining, bitching, and moaning. I was slamming the things he was doing. So he told me about it. He called me aside, and said, "Hey, man, when you get your mother fucking team, you do whatever the fuck you want to do. Until then, you do it the way I tell you to!" Something clicked for me when he said that, and it made so much sense. That's the kind of loyalty and learning they are looking for, because it's not what you are looking for as an assistant coach. This isn't your world. It's his universe. Your head coach must believe that you are fully committed. It's from this experience that I can still vividly recall some workouts back at Douglas High School when only seven players showed up for practice. I walked into Coach Jones's office and asked him, 'Coach, we've only got seven players here. What should I do?' He looked at me and said, 'Coach, just give them your absolute best.'

I was puzzled and asked, 'Why?' Coach Jones replied, 'Well, we may not have enough to line up in a formation, but you can always rely on the dependable ones who are here and need your best.'

That moment stayed with me throughout my career, and I carried it as a guiding principle. I made a promise to myself to always depend on the dependable and rely on the reliable, making sure that the committed young people who are with us understand that I'm equally committed to them. I vowed to give them my best every single day.

You want to make it clear to your head coach that you are there to win. You want both of you to be the best you can be on and off the field. Coach Jones's correction of my behavior aided me for the rest of my career. Since then, I've been a devoted soldier. I was the head coach's stand-in. This was one of the most valuable lessons I could have learned from him.

Loyalty is a rare commodity, and loyal people are difficult to come by. The head coach must have faith that you will communicate his vision to the young men you lead! You can only build a special organization when everyone is on board with the head coach's vision and mission.

Understanding your Head Coach

What do I mean when I say "learn from your head coach?" Investing time in learning how he operates, what his philosophies are, and comprehending his vision. Once you've gotten to know your head coach, your job is to assist him in expanding that vision.

This is why it is critical to work for a head coach in whom you believe and who shares your vision. When an aspect of someone's vision is not similar to or exactly what you want, it's difficult to support it. Without that shared goal, you risk pulling your group of student-athletes in a different direction than the head coach, which can only harm the team as a whole. Therefore, it's in the best interest of the student-athletes for you to understand the head coach's vision and implement it accordingly. One of the first steps in ensuring that you are implementing the head coach's vision is to communicate the same message to your team's locker room. Then, proceed to operate from a position of excellence and professionalism.

Put your best foot forward for the student-athletes in your room by pouring into them with love. Encouraging them in all areas of their lives, watching film, and correcting any mistakes the young men make. As well, as ensuring that they continue to improve and learn how to transfer what they learn in the classroom to the field. Make sure you break things down for them for a week so they really understand what you're saying.

To be a student of the game, you must always be looking for new information about your position. You can begin by observing other teams. Knowing and studying your opponent is an essential part of being a student of the game. You should always try to improve the program with new ideas, but you should also make sure that your ideas align with the vision of the head coach.

Chapter 2

As a Coordinator

Now that you have left your job's comfort zone, it's time to broaden your horizons. Coordinators are in charge of making decisions that have repercussions throughout the organization. You must be able to see the big picture; your team as a whole, you must first get to know it inside and out. Understand the minds of your colleagues, staff, and players.

Take in All the Perspectives

Go meet with other special teams, offensive, and defensive coordinators to share ideas, get feedback, and pick their brains. It is critical to broaden your knowledge so that you can learn how to implement your system and take a holistic approach to your coaching decisions.

Meeting with other coordinators isn't the only way to become well-rounded; going to clinics, visiting different high schools to talk ball, and sitting down with college coaches to learn how to prepare kids for the next level are all part of it.

AS A COORDINATOR

As a coordinator, you must be able to transfer your leadership to the game. Your ability to adjust is critical, you must plan for it. You can have all of your thoughts, ideas, and game plan down to the smallest detail, and then the opposing team changes everything you studied on them. How well can you change your game plan on the fly? Making in-game adjustments allows people to recognize that you are competent and know how to communicate with your staff and players.

It's a different monster when the paper says one thing and your opponent does the exact opposite. You expect them to run one play, but they run another, and you're thinking, "Oh, I've never seen them do that?" Okay, that may hurt you the first time. How do you adjust? How do you communicate? This is why your communication skills must be excellent in order to be an effective coordinator. In the heat of the moment, you're sending instructions to your staff that will eventually reach the ears of your players. It is critical to plan for changes because things do not always go as planned. It will not always be black and white. It's not always going to be that easy.

When mistakes occur, you will be tempted to stick to your well thought-out plan and prove that the time and effort spent developing it was worthwhile. Don't let your ego grow to the point where you need to prove that your plan will work. Your philosophy and decision-making abilities will be harmed, and you will fail to listen to your assistant coaches who are clearly telling you it's time for a change because you are getting your ass kicked. Remember, you've taught them, so be open and receptive to their suggestions. You delegated their responsibilities, and they are the experts in that situation. The trust you've built is reciprocal, you must believe what they're telling you and listen to their feedback. The beauty of working as a team is that you can draw from a variety of perspectives. Make them the expert in different areas of the game plan and you will give them ownership and they will feel apart of the system and this will make the program more transparent.

Outside of game days, listening to your staff's feedback and input is very important as well. We should consistently organize meetings and brainstorm ideas for enhancing team bonding. One of the coach's suggestions was to host events such as barbecues, movie nights, bowling, or playing dodgeball. I believed that these team bonding activities would bring us closer together. I vividly recall a specific Friday when we were playing dodgeball. Among our players, Speedy Noil stood out as one of the best athletes I've ever coached. He found himself as the last man standing on his team, facing five opponents.

In a daring move, Speedy called for a timeout and said, 'I'm going to eliminate all five of you, so you better take your shot now.' I can still remember that moment as if it happened yesterday. The opposing team huddled during the timeout and devised a plan. They decided to count down together, 'One, two, three,' and simultaneously threw their balls at Speedy.

As the countdown ensued, everything seemed to slow down, resembling a scene from The Matrix. Astonishingly, Speedy evaded every ball, except for the very last one, which he caught, with that catch, the player who had thrown the last ball was eliminated. Now, with three balls in his hand and one wedged between his feet, Speedy took precise shots, eliminating each opponent one by one.

AS A COORDINATOR

As we watched from the sideline, we realized that this incredible moment was a turning point for our team bonding. All the players rushed onto the court, exchanging congratulatory embraces. Even the members of the opposing team joined in, sharing the love and camaraderie. These team bonding moments and the lessons they taught us were instrumental in our success.

One of the biggest lessons in becoming a coordinator is not to be afraid to make mistakes. Don't think that mistakes won't happen. You will make the wrong call or the plan will go off the rails. It's imperative that you don't lose your composure and always try to galvanize the troops. Make your staff understand that you will have some casualties in war. Make them realize that it is not how they respond in battle that matters, but how they respond in order to win the war. The more time you and staff are spending time together outside of football will build comradery amongst the unit. T.E.A.M. (Together Everyone Achieves More) is the most important thing we can do.

Aim to Inspire

You must motivate the team, because you are their spokesperson. Whatever side of the ball you're in charge of, whether it's offense, defense, or a special teams unit; they need to see that they can rely on you and your review of what's going to happen during the game.

You used to be the position's head coach, but now you're the voice of the defense or offense. You must be able to motivate those guys so that they will give you their all. Some people believe that motivation is simply a rah-rah speech. It's not about how loud you can scream or how well you can perform various tasks. You use statistics to motivate them. You inspire them by describing past successes or how you got to where you are now.

You cannot defeat the beast of motivation on your own. They don't always want to hear from you about how they can succeed because they know you believe in them. So show them the finished product through the eyes of their peers. Players can benefit from seeing examples of others who have excelled in situations similar to your team's, especially if they come from guys their own age. We can provide numerous examples of challenges that our players may encounter, much like those faced by other young men. It's essential that we demonstrate love and serve as strong role models for our players. Additionally, we should invite our former players to return and share their personal experiences at Karr, highlighting how the program has positively impacted their lives. Sometimes all they need to know is that it is possible. They can then look to you to make it happen.

How do you get a bad team to come to practice every day if you're not having much success? You continue to motivate them and demonstrate the progress they are making. This is where your numbers come into play.

When it's time to take stats to your guys, you have to show them the progress numbers—good and bad. Here's x, y, z. Here's our track record. We achieved a top-ten ranking in the state for our outstanding defensive performance in points allowed on defense, as well as securing the 15th position for points scored on offense. Our history is filled with remarkable success, and we are committed to maintaining this winning tradition. We possess a deep understanding of our strategies, and we are confident that they will continue to yield successful results.

AS A COORDINATOR

Draw attention to specific areas. How much better can we be if we work on these minor details? Turnover must be minimal, or we will compromise on offense. Being explosive, as well as efficient, have all come together. However, you must be able to demonstrate the team's efficiency numbers. When you're winning games, look at your turnover totals and how you've won the turnover battle. When you're losing, look at how many turnovers you're giving up. Your players can spend all day listening to you talk about what needs to be changed, but they want to see the logic behind your instruction. So you must demonstrate, men and women lie, numbers and numbers do not lie.

You can spark some competition once your team understands where they can improve. I believe that challenging them to be better than the guy next to them on a daily basis is the most effective motivator. However, you must reward players who actively work to improve their skills. You cannot tolerate a sluggish mindset. That means players can't tell themselves, "I don't need to practice hard today because they won't play me anyway." No, you motivate with competition and then we use the best guy.

Finding Your Philosophy

As a coordinator, you must be clear about your goals with each decision. While you still follow the head coach's philosophy, you have more leeway with your team's progress. Organize with your staff. What is your philosophy? How do you install your offense or defense? What is your progression? Will you be a run first team or a pass first team? Properly communicating your goals and motivations to your staff is extremely important. You must because it allows the position coaches to function as an extension of you. If they don't understand your message, the other assistants and the head coach may make closed-minded suggestions.

Again, your players and staff must believe in you and trust you. We must always provide young people with a clear understanding of why they are engaging in certain activities. When they grasp the 'why' behind their actions and its significance, they become more motivated to give their best effort. Sometimes, simply clarifying situations can offer a young man a better perspective on their responsibilities. Observing their peers successfully undertake those responsibilities sets a powerful example.

Here's an example from my memory. Korey Williams, a gifted freshman linebacker (usually freshmen didn't start at Karr), displayed exceptional talent on the field. However, I vividly recall a Monday before our first playoff game when I observed him engaged in a heated argument with the coach. I advised him to be quiet and heed the coach's instructions, but he persisted in his disagreement.

Eventually, I decided to intervene and informed Corey that he wouldn't be playing in the upcoming game on Friday. As the game day approached, the coaching staff repeatedly inquired about Korey's participation. Staying resolute, I firmly stated that he would not be playing, and I discouraged further inquiries.

Ultimately, Korey did not participate in the Friday game, which led to our team's loss. Looking back, I acknowledge my own stubbornness in wanting to make a point to both the team and the coaches. After the defeat, I posed a question to the coaches: "Are you willing to lose in order to win?"

AS A COORDINATOR

I emphasized that our focus should extend beyond winning football games; we're here to succeed in the game of life. Not allowing Korey to play set a tone for our program's future, steering us in the right direction. Winning in life takes precedence over winning a football game. It's crucial that our young athletes believe in the values we instill in them because one day, the football field will fade away, and they'll need to secure jobs and provide for their future families. We must ensure they are equipped with effective communication skills, understanding that sometimes listening is the most valuable tool they can possess.

Our commitment to loving and supporting them, giving our all, provides these young individuals with opportunities for great success. Not all of them will go on to play college football, but we can still provide them with a chance to attend college and earn a degree, which can profoundly impact their lives."

When they trust you, they won't question what you're saying. There will be no doubt because they will know that you are well organized, that you are detailed in your decision making, and that you are competent in all of those areas. In order to become a coordinator, you must have a staff and team that trusts and respects you. Having a capable staff will help you get through difficult times. Being on the same page is critical, as it will allow the unit to grow. With growth comes bigger rewards for the entire organization.

Chapter 3

As a Head Coach in High School

Now you are thinking about if you had 100 kids on a team, and you have to make the season for those hundred kids and your twenty-three coaches. Your decisions have a much farther reach. As the head coach of your team, you represent a part of your school's system, so you need to walk side by side with the community and administration. Taking care of your guys involves organizing physicals, birth certificates, shot records, insurance, gear certification, knowing the procedures when a player gets hurt, understanding the rules of recruiting, and much more - If you do it right.

Build Beyond the Team

As a head coach, you need to be in your community. Not only does it strengthen moral support for your team, but it can also encourage

AS A HEAD COACH IN HIGH SCHOOL

business partnerships. You need to be visible, and that requires your players to step up. Community service projects are great for creating positive relationships with the locals. Whether you are going to the elderly-living homes to plant flower beds or reading books to elementary students, your team can make a social impact. You have to get the athletes involved as much as you can. My team would have a clean-up project or go feed the homeless. All of those things are important for the head coach to get out and galvanize the community to come in and let them know that they appreciate it, not only when they come to the games on Friday nights.

Be an advocate for your athletes with sponsorships. It sounds intimidating, but you can find support from almost anywhere, including your town's Wal-Mart, churches, or local mom-and-pop stores. You want to make sure that you are taking the players to different churches where they all feel that they are involved and the church would want to either give money or time to your school. Being involved in the community is very important. Some sponsors may donate money, supplies, or time to your program and school.

At times, Karr didn't have a penny to spare, so we partnered up with Wal-Mart. They built benches at the school and would donate laundry detergent to wash the uniforms, but we also looked locally. The business we washed our uniforms at went on to buy an advertisement in the football program as a way to give back. Just having that relationship in the community is extremely important to make sure that they know that we care about them and we appreciate the support that they give to the young men.

PART 1: HIGH SCHOOL GROWTH

Trust the People in the School

A high school administration includes the principal, assistant principal, athletic directors, and chief academic leaders. You want to make sure that these individuals in the school are all involved in your program. Having the administration involved ensures that they know what your vision is and what the football team will look like in the building. It won't always be easy to get their attention. Outside of your team members, they have many, many more to focus their resources on. You need to prove to them that a mutual relationship of trust can benefit the kids in the classroom and on the football field.

Transparency between the administration and the coach is extremely important. What does that look like? The principal who hired you wants to see some type of structure and discipline. They see the kids more than you will on a daily basis, so an open line of communication can help you better evaluate a player and show the administration a different side of their student. If the administration says your athletes are causing disruptions in the building, they will most likely commit penalties on the field. You want to eliminate penalties as much as you can. An assistant principal may be dealing with day-to-day operations, including behavior issues. You want to let them know that you are backing them in their decision and that you're not going to come to them and say, "Hey, look the other way if James (or any player) does this." You would be undermining their authority and ruining your own reputation at the same time. As a coach, you should be in support of what they are doing. If a student athlete misbehaves and you want to correct it, understand that it will take a united effort. You must yourself: Are you willing to lose in order to win? Winning in life is more important than winning on the field, so we may have to bench some of your better players. In my first year as Head Coach I had to bench my best player Korey Williams (Fr) and the staff didn't believe I would carry it out and we lost the game. But we won in his life and he understands today why we did what we did to save his life! Tough love is needed in our youth lives and we must be consistent in our daily walk of life.

Now, you want to always focus on academics as well. You want the teachers to know that you have their backs. If a player isn't meeting their standards in the classroom, you're not going to play them. This shows that you value their work and the education of your team. Once that trust is built, teachers can help set up tutoring whether it's early in the morning, afterschool, or during their off period.

We tried an after school program where teachers could get paid for tutoring two hours out the day, in the evening, or even in the summertime. That is how we were able to build a relationship. Dave David Johnson used to always say, "Books over ball." So, we make sure that the teachers understand that "books over ball" is the best way to support the players. And when there are less penalties in the school building, there will be less penalties on the field.

Be Prepared for the Worst

The more organized we are in conjunction with our medical staff, the more streamlined our safety precautions will be. Here are steps for being prepared:

- For incoming freshmen, get in contact with the athletic director and have a mass physical every year at the same time. I would get with the medical organization that we partner with and say, "We're going to have physicals on April 1st of every year." Physicals are good for a calendar year, so whoever takes the physical will have completed it for all sports. If you have multiple athletes that play football, basketball, baseball and run track, that physical is good up until then.

- Create a folder with proof of age, a copy of their ID, and proof of residency. You can't always trust that the parents won't bend the truth. They could easily say, "Yeah, he's 15 years old," and in reality he is 17 years old, meaning he is ineligible. When having that folder together with physicals and personal eligibility forms, you will be organized for the association and for any emergencies.

- In that same folder, you'll also need to have an informational card of relevant health needs (like food allergies, grass allergy, and lotions). We carry that physical form with us wherever we go. If someone were to get hurt, that physical form we will give to the doctors all the information they need to treat our players correctly.

- When traveling, it's best to know where the local hospitals are and its distance from the school, in case of an emergency.

More than Eligibility—Grade Point Average

The same folders holding players' medical and verification information should also hold their updated academic information—most importantly, their grade point average. This single number indicates how well they are keeping up with their school work, which affects more than just their ability to play. Each student has to maintain a certain grade point average.

Some states require a 1.5 GPA, but we typically aim for a 2.5 GPA to ensure that if a player is fortunate enough to play college football, they are also academically prepared. If they are not fortunate enough to continue their athletic career at a high level, a 2.5 GPA can get them into a college or university.

Your player's core grade point average should match his or her ACT/SAT score. The NCAA uses a sliding scale, so if you have a low GPA, you can compensate with a higher ACT/SAT score. On the other hand, the higher their GPA, the lower your score. However, you cannot allow your players to place all of their hopes in the ACT/SAT. Even if his GPA is impressive, a player's test scores may not be reflective of his GPA because he does not test well. Finally, the more your players concentrate on achieving a respectable GPA, the less pressure there is to achieve a perfect score.

For many, becoming a head coach will be the most difficult challenge. If you're not aware of the additional responsibilities outside of running drills, it will be confusing and possibly overwhelming. Many of you simply want to coach football, but managing your players' education, health, and eligibility is a critical part of your job.

Prioritize Injury Protection

After you've dealt with your off-field safety precautions, it's time to focus on your injury prevention on the field. It is critical to teach your players proper positioning and to strengthen their bodies to withstand impact; their equipment is a player's first line of defense.

A certification company comes in to inspect helmets and pads to see if they need to be reconditioned or if they are unusable. Both of those pieces of equipment must be inspected on a yearly basis. Keep track of the condition and age of your helmets and shoulder pads to stay ahead of the game. If you bought twenty-five sets of new shoulder pads and then the next coach came in and bought more, the gear will have different expiration dates. A detailed record of which helmets and pads were purchased on which dates will assist you in staying organized and will benefit future coaches.

The protective gear will eventually lose its durability, so it's critical to keep that liability under control. If an athlete suffers a catastrophic injury while wearing an outdated helmet, you are inviting lawsuits. More importantly, faulty helmets or pads endanger athletes, and you must ensure that they are kept safe.

Nailing Your Form 48H

The NCAA makes the List of Approved Core Courses (Form 48H) for your school available online. If you truly believe in your players' ability to play college football, start the paperwork as soon as possible. You should have a plan in place for everything starting in the athlete's freshman year, according to the form 48H. "Tim could be in his junior year," you can't wait to say. You must tell yourself that they are all good and that you will prepare him for the next level so that his freshman and sophomore years are not so detrimental that he cannot recover.

You must also understand how to add and subtract from your 48H form. For example, if you teach journalism at your school, you must include it in your English department on your 48H. You must also understand how to add and subtract from your 48H form. For example, if you teach journalism at your school, you must include it in your English department on your 48H. The more classes you have on the 48H, the more opportunities athletes will have to take classes. Some players may be weak in certain areas, but they are strong in others, which you can highlight with the form. Your 48H should be up to date, and all of the classes listed on the form should be approved. They are unable to change the classes once they have been approved.

Recognize that the 48H is your bible, not the NCAA's. It can only highlight what your school has to offer in terms of curriculum. Now, if you provide the NCAA with all of the necessary information in your curriculum and course details, the NCAA will most likely approve it. It's all about presenting your school's offerings in the best possible light. Don't even think about lying about your courses or descriptions because the NCAA will see right through you. You must ensure that all of these things are in place so that the young men in your care have a variety of options. Don't limit their ability to accomplish their goals.

As a high school student, we cannot simply think of core courses as taking four English, four math, four sciences, and four social studies.

What can you do to expand on those classes? Why only four for each? Your players can broaden their horizons by taking new courses that complement their application. They are only required to take the core classes, but you don't want to restrict them to only sixteen. You want to broaden their options as much as possible, which includes looking beyond the requirements for curriculum.

Once the senior year begins, the first ten courses are locked. If your player is in their senior year, they should have taken three classes in each subject area. Then you realize what can be added to it, and you want to get the highest grades in those classes, even though you only have ten left. Then you have a wide range of classes on your 48H. The next six classes he takes will be crucial because grades cannot be changed once they are locked in. You can't simply retake a class that he's already passed, so you'll need to be very familiar with how to add and subtract from the 48H. That will benefit you and the young men you are in charge of.

Building Culture

Building a culture requires the trust that you will not only speak about it but will also live it. You are a living example of it. Mutual understanding is the only way to build a foundation of trust, so you must make the effort to connect.

Charge each position coach a day to spend at your house just hanging out and getting to know each other on a personal level. Create bonding activities for your staff that aren't centered on the game, such as organizing a group lunch or making time to hang out on weekends. This not only strengthens your staff's relationships, but it also helps to foster a holistic mindset. Coaches can gain a better understanding of their peers' perspectives and begin to incorporate them into their decision-making process. Please feel free to publicize these bonding activities. You can have pictures of you and your staff hanging out to show the young men that you're building a strong unit through bonding activities.

Camps are an excellent opportunity for your players to bond. The guys must share a dorm with a guy they don't know, and sharing that space can help break down those early barriers. They need to know who he is, who his family is, where he came from, what he likes and dislikes before they leave that dorm. This is where some of the most genuine friendships have developed.

Some players' coaches are likely the only male figures in their lives. The coach will have a significant influence on the young men's sensibilities, so you must ensure that the culture is appropriate. Building a trust system is the first step. We're not just going to talk about being a family; you'll be a part of it. A family gathers to eat, pray, and stay together. Some people use the term "family" too casually when it should be lived and discussed. Your players need to know that their coach will care for them. My players continue to send me text messages on Father's Day and my birthday. They will remember it if you create a true family out of your team.

Furthermore, have core values in which you believe and make the guys live them. However, you must set a good example. You can't just tell them to do one thing while doing another. This is

where the adage "Do as I say, not as I do" comes up short. For example, if you tell them not to smoke weed and you have guys who will continue to smoke weed with no consequences. That is not a good combination, and we must be able to separate the two.

Then it spreads to the field. Your children play hard, but they are respectful to everyone, regardless of which side they are on. That is, they are not using profanity on the field and instead respond to the coach and referee with yes sir or no sir. If they have a minor altercation and the referee orders them to be quiet, their response should be yes sir, and they should remain silent. When someone says something nice to you, it's the ultimate compliment: "Your children are hardworking and disciplined. Keep up the good work; they have structure." That's what you want people to say about you when they're watching you. When the team's respect and dignity carry over from the field, you know the culture is real and sustainable. Building that culture was a top priority for me when I first started out. I wanted to create a program rather than be a one-hit wonder. That is how you build a winning culture if you want to be a consistent winner year after year.

Supporting Recruiters

When a coach visits your school, you must understand that his time is valuable. He may be attempting to visit twelve schools in one day, so it is your responsibility to stay organized. I put every senior on a spreadsheet with all of a player's information when making a recruiting list. Height, weight, address, email, parents' names, data, transcripts, ACT scores, and contact information with a picture are all included on the sheet. I also have a copy of their transcript to go along with it. If you're prepared when that college coach walks in and says, "Coach, here you go. Here are my team members. Examine the transcripts and everything." Now he's going to call a colleague and say, "Listen, man, stop by this school; the coach is well-organized. You won't waste time because he has everything organized." Your preparation can demonstrate to recruiters and coaches that you value their time and the process.

College coaches can see what he looks like, how tall he is, and evaluate his prospects with one simple step on your part. If you want to reduce your paperwork, go digital. You can do this by making a card with a link to your recruiting department's website that you can hand out to the coach. This makes it much easier for them to look through all of your eligible players. When that recruiter walks onto your field, it is your responsibility as a head coach to be properly prepared to increase the chances of your athletes being recruited.

Choosing Your Staff

Hiring is extremely difficult because you want to be extremely selective as the head coach. I believe that men make the mistake of hiring their friends. I want to hire the best candidate for the job.

The most important quality I look for in a coach is loyalty. Loyalty to both me and the other players. We genuinely care about our children, so he must be committed to them. If he knows some football that's a plus, but he doesn't have to be a football guru, because he'll be an extension of me as the head coach. I can teach him so that he has the tools he needs to succeed. Loyalty is about being present for your coach and team, not about your level of knowledge. Your availability and accountability are more important to me than your football knowledge.

These are the qualities I look for in a coach. They manifest themselves in various ways: how they carry themselves, if they have a family, or if they are single. All of these factors influence the hiring process. You put guys in a position to continue to be successful once you've found that special combination of loyalty and accountability.

You want to keep the coaches, but how do you go about doing so? You create a work environment that encourages their development. You don't want a micromanaged work environment that is oppressive. Your coaches' unique talents are there to elevate your team, so you must let them do the work. You entrust your coaching staff with appropriate responsibilities and hold them accountable. The give and take shows your guys that their expertise is valued, which encourages them to return the favor by remaining loyal to you and the team. That is how you develop a good coaching staff and foster camaraderie.

I can recall the time when I approached Desmond Moore and asked him to coach wide receivers. He hesitated, saying, 'Coach, I've never coached football before.' I responded, 'Perfect.' Despite the puzzled look on his face, I explained that his loyalty and dedication were the two most important qualities I valued. I assured him that I would teach him the game of football. He not only embraced the opportunity but also excelled in guiding the young men in our program. This is what it's all about!

Chapter 4

Building Team Trust

Team camaraderie will help boost morale, but the lines between coach and teammate can be easily blurred. It is critical that your players understand that you are not a friend to them. You have to be a coach. Personally, I prefer that my players respect me rather than like me, and I strongly advise you to do the same.

Because there's times when you are only a few years older than your players, this message is critical for young coaches. I've been in situations where the age difference was so small that players regarded me as a big brother. You must, however, learn how to convey the message: I am not your big brother, uncle, or father. My name is Coach. My players understand that authoritative dynamic better now that I'm more experienced. When I was younger, I had to make sure they understood that our relationship could be wonderful without crossing the line of strict coach-player rapport. Set the tone early on.

Once that bond is established, you will be able to support your players on and off the field. My mentoring begins at home. I make sure that my players come over to my house to see what it's like in a family-structured environment. Make your players feel safe and don't betray their trust. Slowly, they will respond to this stability by telling you about events at home or challenges they are facing. It is your responsibility to listen to the players and learn about them. This will allow you to look at them and tell when something is wrong. Now, you call them in and talk to them, because you've built a trusting relationship. They can open up to you as a coach and mentor and express their hardships. Your players should feel at ease coming into your office and discussing family, school, or relationship issues. The line between friendship and a coach-player relationship is very thin, and you cannot cross the line. Get to know your players as individuals, and build a close bond that they could trust you while maintaining the respect and honor of a coach.

Academics

While making it to the college or professional level of football is not impossible, it does require a certain talent that not everyone possesses. As a coach, you must continue to emphasize the importance of academics in order to ensure that your players understand that their football careers may have an expiration date. Many of these players will be first-generation college graduates who have dedicated their lives to this sport, so it is your responsibility to bring a Plan B to the forefront of their career planning.

This is where your faith comes into play. Knowing about their personal lives will provide you with insight into the type of support and guidance they need to receive, as well as how your mentorship fits. We must emphasize the value of obtaining a degree and change the narrative of their family history.

Chapter 5

Building Relationships with College Coaches

Building relationships with college coaches can be difficult for some guys, particularly those who lack certain social skills. There are, however, excellent techniques available to you that do not necessitate an abundance of charisma. Just keep in mind that each college coach is unique. Some are willing to assist anyone, while others prefer to remain private. I'm a little unusual in that I don't mind giving guys my phone number on a regular basis. While you may not be able to establish that level of communication with every college coach, it is certainly possible to establish a solid relationship.

Speak the Truth

How do you gain the trust of college coaches in a relationship? When they come in to recruit your student athlete, you tell them the *whole* truth. You

BUILDING RELATIONSHIPS WITH COLLEGE COACHES

don't try to oversell a player in order to persuade them of the caliber of your team. If the coach discovers that a player lacks the abilities you described to him, you become the boy who cried wolf. They won't believe you when you really do have a good player.

They will always contact you if you continue to have good players. However, if you have good judgment, they will contact you when you don't have a player and say, "What about this other kid from another school? After playing against him, what are your thoughts on him? Just give me your thoughts." Even if the path is not yours, pointing them in the right direction demonstrates to them that they can trust you to prioritize their time. And if your intuition is correct, coaches will say, "This guy has a keen sense of talent. He knows what talent is and will continue to tell us the truth."

Start the Conversation

As time goes on, use that foundation of trust to develop a deeper relationship. You don't necessarily have to talk about football. When a coach comes to visit your school to recruit, ask him how his family is doing, if he's married, or how his family deals with the college day atmosphere. Invite them to dinner or for a drink. Now the coach can see you in a different setting. He needs to know that you see him as more than just a means to an end for your player's football careers. When trying to make a relationship with a coach, shoot them a text on Father's Day or tell his wife you said Happy Mother's Day that's how relationships are built. While you will be tempted to push things, don't overdo it. Let the relationship come naturally.

Don't be afraid to pick up the phone and reach out for an honest conversation. This is the opportune time to receive guidance. Don't just be on the phone shooting the shit and wasting time, get to the point. "Coach, I was curious about how you would handle an athlete in this situation?" It can be a good situation or a bad, either way it's asking for advice. You are trying to prepare your young men to go to college and no one will know better than the college coach on the other end of the line. When I say make contact, I don't mean to call somebody every day because these guys have jobs and families too. Hopefully within the time frame of you communicating with the coach and his visits to your campus, you will form a relationship.

The best way to solidify your relationship is to establish that you are dependable in person. You should work camps, so they can see you actually working. If you're lucky, they might just see you as a guy they want to be able to hire one day. Sit one-on-one with the coach and let them know how much football you understand. Don't be afraid to not know something because high school and college football are a little different just like college and the NFL are different. You have to be able to incorporate things that college coaches are doing to what you're doing on a high school level just to simplify and make it work.

When the timing is right, let them know that you do have interest in moving up to the college level. What do I need to do to get into college coaching? What are some of my options?" Don't ask them, "Can you give me a job?" I don't think that's the way to go. I never asked those guys about getting a job. That wasn't my M.O. I never got into coaching for money, I was trying to impact lives and build productive citizens. I believe there is

BUILDING RELATIONSHIPS WITH COLLEGE COACHES

a fine line of asking for a job and saying you are interested in potentially coaching in college football one day. Some college coaches may give you some pointers.

They may tell you some do's and don'ts just to help you along the way. Some coaches are guarded in that area because sometimes they're afraid you will come to take their job. They don't want to help other coaches out, but I'm a little different. I want to help as many guys as I can because I'm not going to be a coach forever, and they're going to need the next generation of guys who come in and continue to build legacies and help these young men out as best they can.

Part 2

COLLEGE GROWTH

Chapter 6

How to Prepare for College Coaching Interviews

You may have had a few interviews as a junior high and high school coach, but college is a completely different beast to master. As you look for a higher-level job, keep in mind that opportunities are scarce. At the peak of the season, demand exceeds supply. You must go in there and convince the staff why you will be an integral part of their success in the development of the young men that you will be leading. "That guy is a good fit for us," the coach should say at the end of your interview. "He is exactly what we require. He's someone who will be able to help assist us along the way."

In the days leading up to the big interview day, have someone give you mock interviews. You don't need to go daily, but at least once or twice a month leading up to it. Be ready so you don't have to get ready at the last minute. I used to always have my guys do mock interviews. The mock interview let you see what you're doing and gives an opportunity to receive constructive criticism from your peers so that you can be prepared for whatever someone tells you. We don't have all the answers but we can always learn by being seekers of knowledge. You need to continue to enhance your craft, perfect it, and master it. In that regard, it is important that we get among our peers and be able to be comfortable speaking to others in an uncomfortable environment.

Dress to Impress

If you want to make a great impression, your confidence and reliability should show from the first second you walk through that door for the interview. Your clothing should consist of tidy business attire that matches the professional setting. Swap out your blazer and jeans for a button-up shirt with a tie. A suit is even better. It's all about how you're going to be able to go in there and impress them.

When they see you in your suit and tie, they'd say "This gentleman or woman can represent me when I'm not around." Your appearance will not only play a part on the field but also when meeting athletes and interacting with their families. Therefore, it's imperative to dress well in order to properly represent the organization. Dress for success with a well-groomed hairstyle and facial hair. Remember, you're not going to a club or fashion show. You're going into a professional interview, and you want to be dressed appropriately for that.

Go Above and Beyond

Now that you are looking professional, you need to know what to bring with you to that interview. You may go into your interview and experience the standard question-and-answer model, but you should also be prepared with a presentation that lets them know who you are. I've found that the best way to highlight your body of work and personal attributes is through a well-crafted slide presentation. Highlight key areas of your knowledge and experience that you elaborate on because you want the interviewers to have your undivided attention. Your presentation does not have to be wordy. You don't want them to get lost in long-winded sentences or tune you out. When you can only read from the board rather than speak directly to them, that can easily happen!

Within that presentation, include the following:

- **Who you are**
- **Where are you from**
- **What you're currently doing**
- **Your family dynamics** (which consist your status as married or single, kids or no kids, and other home life details)

    **Once you have laid the foundations for who you are with the presentation, you can better expand on your skills as a coach.

- **How much you know about the position that you're interviewing for, including the entire offense or the entire defense, or whatever side of the ball that you will be.** Be prepared for the interviewer to say, "What do you know about this position?" Tell them what you know and *stand* by what you know, but don't come off as a know-it-all if they do things differently. If you don't know something, say you don't know it and move forward. These coaches can smell a pretender a mile away, so you need to make sure that you're being honest.

- **A video of you actually coaching the position you're interviewing for or coaching through the drill work you are possibly going to be doing.** This gives them a direct look into your style of coaching.

- **A list of the top players of that area for that upcoming class.** With this addition, they will know that you're prepared to go out, identify the talent, and go through an excellent evaluation process. (Be prepared to explain to them how you are going to go out and build team relationships so you can get those athletes to execute the overall game plan.

- **How you structure your team meeting rooms and communicate with the young men on the team.** For my team meetings, I try to have my objectives on the board to describe the goal for that day. We have a package that I go over that is correlated to the objectives. Then, everyone is going to watch the film and all three of those tasks are going to tie into what we're going to be working on during practice. I clearly present the day's goals to my players, give them supportive information, and then create objectives that help them progress. You need to decipher how you want to teach your student athletes to address their learning styles and push them in the right direction. You've got a plan for your athletes, and the interviewers will take note.

While you want to demonstrate your ability to make connections with your players during the interview, you shouldn't give off the impression that you like to be their best friend. You have to convince the coaching staff that you're going to be able to control your room. How are you going to go in and set your structure and discipline?

Inevitably, issues will arise and you need to showcase that you'll handle these delicate situations. How do you control those to convince the coaching staff that you're going to be able to control your room? How are you going to go in and set your structure and discipline? Inevitably, issues will arise and you need to showcase that you'll handle these delicate situations. How do you control those things? Control comes in academics first and foremost by making sure that your guys are accountable for going to class and maintaining their grades. The next form of control is socialization. Young men are influenced by many different people during this formative time in their lives, so you must ensure that they are making good social decisions while you're away from the building. The third form is managing the playing time with fairness in mind. Playing favorites shows that your decisions can't be relied on. This is a huge part of being able to show your interview that you are well aware of the dynamics in your room and that you can confidently handle it.

In your interview, also show your playbook that you usually run at your current school. You want to be able to show that you have that knowledge and let them know that you are a student of the game. This is how you show your progression of work and your program. You don't necessarily want them to think you are coming in to change what they are doing— but you want them to be aware of what you are capable of doing. If you really want to make an impact in your interview, being knowledgeable of the university or the institution that you're going to work for can push you to the top of eligible job candidates. Take note of what their record has been for the last 10 years. This will tell you if they have a winning program on the dynamics of who the coach is and his background. If you did your research correctly, you should know the head coach, the coaching staff, what they've been implementing, and their different statistical records from the last five years. It may seem like a lot of work to put in for just an interview, but if you really want it, prepare fully!

In my opinion, a great presentation shows your preparedness, emphasizes your knowledge of the game, and gives them all the information they need about who you are as a person.

Chapter 7

As a College Coach

Everything is on a larger scale in college football. More players are competing for your team, more parents rely on your integrity, and many more people are evaluating your progress. In my case, the running backs at the University of Louisiana worked hard regardless of who was on the field. That was my reflection! Make sure your team reflects your persona. They must adopt your teachings and possess the same abilities in order to be the most dominant player on the field and the most dominant student in the classroom. As well as being one of the most influential and well-rounded people in a community.

Creating Connection on Whole New Level

Once on a college coaching staff, demonstrate your devotion to the head coach. From controlling your room to representing him in the community to being a university ambassador, you will be an extension of the head coach. He must have faith that you will embrace his philosophy

AS A COLLEGE COACH

and ideas. That will be very important for you to keep that job; loyalty goes a long way.

Again, you must be a developer of your players both on and off the football field. You must establish relationships with these young men and demonstrate that they can rely on you. You'll be seeing these players on a daily basis for the next four years, so it's your responsibility to develop the entire young man, not just his athletic abilities. In my opinion, off the field is more important than on the field. You don't want any secrets or surprises off the field, so it's critical to have that relationship that allows them to come to you about anything and everything. "I don't want any surprises now," I tell them, "so please come to me before anything happens."

Then, you want to develop the best students by focusing on their studies in order to ensure that they graduate from college. During the recruiting process, you will discover that parents rely on you to guide their son's academic endeavors. It is essential that you honor their request and their confidence in your ability to lead. Football coaches are plentiful, but can you be a *builder* of men? Are you capable of producing productive citizens, better husbands, better friends, better coworkers, better sons, and better fathers for the world? That is the key to positive development in which I am most proud of myself and what I do. Exemplify your teachings so that they can put those values into action and become trustworthy young men.

Self-Evaluation

Strong communication and connection begin with you. Begin building your reputation once you are confident in your own philosophy and abilities. You want to ensure that people know you are a good person and that you develop good people as a result. I always tell people that you can be a great football coach and a terrible person, but it doesn't end well. I'd rather be a great human being and a person of integrity and honor than try to climb the ladder and harm others in the process.

If I haven't been clear in previous chapters about the importance of following rules with integrity, I want to be clear now. Your decisions affect your integrity, you must be very knowledgeable about the rules and regulations. Making sure you're following the rules and not breaking any laws will protect you from potential defamation of your character. This is especially important in recruiting and practice. These things are constantly evolving, and the rules change frequently. If I have any questions, I always go back to my rulebook or check my compliance.

Being well-versed in NCAA rules and regulations is the only way to properly carry out the tasks required to continue to be successful in this business.

Chapter 8

What To Look For When Recruiting

You'd better be an excellent recruiter! I cannot emphasize this enough. We are nothing without players. You can think that your cone drills are good and you're catching the ball, but assembling your ideal team requires real skill. You must recruit quality players. Finding those guys is only possible when you can trust your eyes. If you want to stay in this business, your excellent recruiting must bring in quality young men with great character, integrity, and athletic ability who can elevate your game.

So, how do you become an effective recruiter? You must be knowledgeable about your field and capable of recruiting your position. It will be pivotal that you are familiar with every good football player in your area and what that person can offer to your program.

The attributes of the players must be a good fit for what you're trying to accomplish with your head coach's vision. How are you going to

WHAT TO LOOK FOR WHEN RECRUITING

improve that by bringing in a quality player? Now, you have to also know your level of play. A player must be able to keep up with the rest of the team in order to contribute on the field as a whole. On the other hand, you shouldn't waste time chasing ghosts by recruiting guys above your level. You must do your homework to ensure that he is able to go out and play.

Once you've determined that a person is talented enough to play and fits your level, you must ensure that his grades are in order. That is the first thing we must consider to ensure he has a chance to compete in the NCAA. The ideal candidate possesses both talent and education. With that, only one thing could stand in his way: his personality. It takes more than one conversation with an athlete to get a full picture of his personality. You can learn about the athlete's character by speaking with his family, seeing what his home life is like, and speaking with school administrators who have interacted with the young man. Whether it's his teachers, administrators, coaches, custodians, cafeteria staff, or bus drivers. Anyone who comes into contact with this young man is important because they see how he acts outside of football. If you skip this crucial step and bring in someone who lacks the character that you believe is appropriate for your program, the clash could devastate the culture.

You must ensure that you conduct a thorough investigation into a young man and his background. No matter how talented he is, if his character and disposition are not compatible with the culture that your head coach is attempting to establish, he will not be a good fit. It's like trying to fit a square peg into a round hole. You can't force it.

It will take time and effort to find the right fit for a recruit.

Here are some tips:

1. Be able to identify the young man at an early age.

2. Start building a relationship with him and his family. That's how you go about really knowing who the young men are that you're trying to recruit.

3. Your goal must be bigger than just recruiting. It's about relationships that you're making inside of your recruitment. That's going to be a deal that we have to make sure that we identify on a regular basis.

4. You have to make sure that the family and your recruit know that you want to make sure their son graduates from college and gets his degree along with developing him as a football player. Getting the parents' trust is extremely important. They are trusting you with their most prized possession.

The 40 - 12 Rule

When recruiting, you must be truthful with the young men. They have 52 weeks in a year and will be playing football 12 of those weeks. I always ask the men and their families about the 40-12 rule. They are leaving their homes to pursue their dreams of attending college, playing Division I football, and potentially earning a chance to play in the NFL. That is something you can accomplish in 12 weeks. When there is a home game and your family is unable to attend while the local guys get to see their families. You must return to your dorm room, are your recruits considering this? They must be able to go through the day without seeing family or old friends. The ability and willingness to make new friends and develop interests outside of sports demonstrates resilience. What will they do for the other 40 weeks? Encourage them to consider the question, "Would I attend this university if I didn't play football?" Because football is only a minor component of what they do. How can they have an impact on the community during the 40 weeks they are not playing football?

That 40-12 rule extends beyond their four-year decision. Joining the football team means you've become a part of the university's history. How often will you return to the community where you began your athletic and academic careers in the next 40 years? The decision to attend your school implies that they intend to be a part of the university for a lifetime, not just for the next few years.

The Coaches' Test

Every year, coaches are required to take a test before hitting the road at the start of the season to ensure they are up to date on the latest guidelines and restrictions. So you'll have to take the test twice a year to recruit during the spring and fall evaluations. It will cover a wide range of recruiting-related topics, so don't put it off. While you must understand the specifics, I can give you a general idea of what to expect.

There are specific times when you can have contact or evaluations. Contact occurs when you are able to physically speak with the young men and their families. You can conduct in-person home visits and build relationships. When evaluating a student athlete, you can only observe him or her at practice or during a game without making direct contact with that person. Your phone calls and messages with the prospective player are also recorded, so it's critical to follow the rules of more casual communication. Prepare for changes and restrictions to keep you from unknowingly violating rules and allowing you to perform your duties with confidence.

You are now held to a higher standard because any infraction can be linked to your head coach. Nobody is going to hire someone who gets violations on a regular basis because they will eventually suspend the head coach for allowing it to happen.

Managing Your Room

Let's say your recruits are now officially players! What should you do now? Similarly to high school coaching, you must become deeply involved in your players' development. You must teach them how to be a student athlete, which includes prioritizing and managing their time in order to maximize their abilities both on and off the football field. That includes a daily routine as well as what he does to develop on the field. That is forcing him to practice in a specific manner because practice performance is game day reality, and we must instill that in him so that he can practice at a high level on a daily basis.

Then we must teach each player how to be a student of the game by watching film and recognizing tendencies in his opponent that can benefit him and his teammates. For example, before I watch the entire piece that we put together with our game plan, I make a schedule for splitting up field sections of the film to analyze more closely. If you do this with your men, it will help them develop as football players by giving them routines and keeping them on track to do those things on time.

WHAT TO LOOK FOR WHEN RECRUITING

Finally, you must ensure that you are managing the egos within your room, as everyone was being told that they were excellent during recruitment. On the front end of recruiting, I let them know that they're going to have to compete every single day. Each young man wants to contribute, but he also does not want to face the harsh realities of not consistently performing at a high level. What I'm curious about is whether a player will be a good teammate. "Are you going to participate in community service or pick up trash in the locker room?" I wonder. "Will you be on any special teams? Will you be the best blocker in the room?" A player can do all of that without even touching the football.

You must be able to manage their disappointment and let them know that they can contribute to the team in some capacity, whether it's scoring touchdowns, blocking for teammates, making a special teams tackle, or being supportive of the young man who may be better than them at the time. You want to ensure your players think like this: "I don't want to lose focus on the team by focusing on myself." Make sure everyone in your room is rooting for one another while also contributing in their own unique way.

Chapter 9

Mentorship

Finding a Mentor

Reaching out to a mentor can make all the difference when you are ready to advance but are unsure how to do so. You must first find the right person. It's easy to seek advice from the most popular person. However, that person will not have enough time to truly guide you to your objectives. You do not want to work with a mentor who does not provide you with advice on a daily or monthly basis, because everyone's time is valuable.

Furthermore, you must find someone who will be completely honest with you. For example, my previous mentors always advised me to conduct myself in a certain manner in order to be recognized as one of the best coaches in the industry. What does this imply? You must be on time, organized, well-dressed, and articulate. These lessons, however, did not come from my best friend or favorite coworker. Because your mentor will

MENTORSHIP

be guiding you in a new direction, they must be someone you admire for their wisdom and integrity, which they will pass on to you.

You can always find a mentor who is not in your field and can provide you with a fresh perspective on how to apply your skills. I've had mentors who don't coach football but provide spiritual guidance and others who provide life insight. As a result, your mentors can come from a variety of backgrounds other than football. It's beneficial to have someone who is also a coach in the sport of football, but you also need someone who is not in the industry to give you advice on how to advance your career and meet your life goals. Burton Burns has been my coach and mentor since I was 15 years old. He is a man of intensity, discipline, and one of the most realest individuals I've ever had the privilege to meet.

Mentoring Players

I make it my mission to know every student on a team by name so they know our relationship extends beyond practices and games and that I will treat them as such. That mentorship means a lot to the young men because they know I'll be there for them both on and off the field. If you truly care about your players, mentoring them will come naturally.

Whether your players approach you for advice or simply observe your actions, you are influencing their moral compass. You must be a mentor or a role model on a consistent basis so that you do not put yourself in a position where they could say, "You didn't do it, Coach. How can you hold me accountable if you're not accountable yourself?" These young men look to you to set a good example, so demonstrate what a good man does.

It is not always necessary to express your values verbally. To be able to say, "Hey, come on in and talk to me," you must have an open door policy. They may not always accept you at first. You can, however, reach out to those you believe could benefit from your guidance, such as young men you were unable to recruit or others who have looked to you as a role model. An open door policy allows them to come in and express their feelings. For example, a reliable wide receiver may come into my office complaining about his lack of playing time after suffering several injuries leading up to his final year. Now that some of the younger players have developed, he claims that his seniority earns him that time on the field.

"You can't say, 'I've been here for so long, I should automatically play,'" I'd tell the young man. That is not the way it works." Football is a production-based business, and the player cannot contribute as he previously did. I would remove him from the game because it is in the best interests of the team. This is where your body language and demeanor come into play.

The wide receiver is not getting what he wants, but he can get what he needs with your help. I would tell the player that he should be doing everything he can to make it difficult for me to not put him in because of his outstanding performance or the manner in which he has practiced. When your players feel comfortable discussing their concerns with you, they can trust that you are looking out for their best interests. That is the attitude you will have toward mentorship. A great mentor shows the child the way rather than telling him what he wants to hear.

Sometimes players don't want to hear the truth, and they expect me to be the person who completely agrees with them. When I know they're

MENTORSHIP

wrong, it's my responsibility to make them look in the mirror and realize the truth hurts sometimes, but it's what's needed. It may sound cliche, but the truth makes you free—so I try to keep an open door policy for every student on the team.

Chapter 10

Networking

Jason Phillips served as a pivotal mentor for me, particularly teaching me the value of networking at conventions. He told me that I should put a list together of all the guys in this industry that I have respect for or who's succeeding at one of my weaknesses. While at a convention, I'd seek them out. Sometimes, it would be as simple as a handshake and quick introduction. I'd let them know who I am, where I coach at, and that I respect and admire what they are doing. I'd then follow this up by asking if there are opportunities for me to visit their school and be a fly on the wall during meetings with staff, position meetings, or coordinator meetings. The short conversations would allow me to visit every one of those guys on the list and learn. At the next convention, I'd do it all again.

I encourage you to dive into this process. You're not necessarily networking to get a job, you're networking to advance your special abilities or knowledge of the game so you can be the best at what you do. If something was to come out of it, great, but remember that's not why you're actually going to sit down and pick those guys' brains. It's just about being able to call someone and ask questions like, *How do you attack this coverage? What do you think about this front? How do you attack this front? What are the things that cause problems for you?* Having general conversations with people in this field of business can go a very long way in this industry.

Here's a recapped shortlist of how to kickoff your networking:

1. Put a list together of all the coaches in this industry that you have respect for or who's succeeding at one of your weaknesses.

2. Make a list of conventions happening this year or next, and plan to attend all of them.

3. When you meet the coaches on your list, tell them who you are, where you coach at, and that you respect and admire what they are doing.

4. Ask if it's possible for you to visit their school and be a fly on the wall during staff meetings, position meetings, or coordinator meetings.

Chapter 11

Finding the Right Partner

Dedicating this chapter to my incredible wife, Denise, this is a tribute to her unwavering support throughout my journey as a college football coach. It's a story of finding the perfect life partner, someone who not only understands the demands of this profession but also embraces it as their own. The importance of choosing the right spouse cannot be underestimated in a career as demanding as college coaching.

When I transitioned from coaching high school football to the college ranks, I realized that this decision wouldn't just impact me; it would profoundly affect my family, especially my wife. She was not just supportive; she was all in. She understood that my dreams were becoming our dreams, and my realities were becoming our realities. For us to thrive, we needed a strong support system in place, one where she felt safe and valued.

FINDING THE RIGHT PARTNER

Our journey began in Ruston, Louisiana, 11 years ago. It was a challenging transition into the unknown. Balancing a coaching profession and family life required careful navigation. I wanted my wife to know that she was more important than football, but I also needed to provide for our family. We've been married for 22 years, and my coaching career has been a constant presence in our lives. Thankfully, Denise embraced football as much as she loved me, and it created a unique bond between us.

Being a football wife is no easy task. There are long periods of separation, and she needed a deep understanding of my profession. We ensured she had a job and a sense of independence, not just to occupy her time but also to have her own identity. It was vital for our relationship to maintain balance.

Our journey led us to Louisiana Tech, where we experienced both highs and lows. We celebrated victories, but more importantly, we grew closer in our marriage, learning to handle separations and constant travel. Effective communication became our lifeline, enabling us to make it work.

As we continued to progress in this unpredictable profession, new opportunities arose. When we received a job offer from Texas Tech University, my wife's immediate "Yes" showed the support we needed. She didn't have to leave her comfort zone, and we were closer to family and friends.

But life had its challenges. In 2017, my wife was diagnosed with stage four breast cancer. We faced this trial head-on, just as she had supported me in my coaching journey. The way she handled this adversity with strength and resilience was awe-inspiring.

During her treatments, the coaching staff, including Coach Kingsbury and the Texas Tech family, provided unwavering support. They ensured a smooth transition of medical insurance and helped us throughout the process. The University Medical Center in Lubbock was phenomenal, and we felt like we had a second family supporting us.

As the season continued, and her cancer became more aggressive, we had to make the tough decision to move closer to family for additional support. Transitioning to the University of Louisiana, we once again faced the challenges of relocation and medical care coordination. However, we were determined to overcome them together.

This chapter is a testament to the importance of choosing a life partner who shares your vision and is willing to stand by your side through thick and thin. The life of a college coach has its ups and downs, but having a supportive spouse makes all the difference. It's a partnership where there is no "I," only "we."

Our journey has been far from perfect, filled with trials, vulnerabilities, and moments of uncertainty. Yet, we've learned to navigate through it all by keeping our priorities straight, nurturing our relationship, and being each other's biggest supporters.

So, to all aspiring college coaches, remember this: choose a partner who understands the challenges ahead, someone who will be your rock during the rocky roads of your coaching career. Find a soulmate who shares your dreams and aspirations, and together, you can conquer anything life throws your way.

You must also be highly supportive of your spouse's goals and ambitions. Grant them the freedom to pursue their dreams and have their own. Our spouses often make significant sacrifices to support us in our endeavors. Show them even more love and appreciation, as their unwavering support allows us to grow in this industry.

Quick Do's and Don'ts for Coaches

Do:

1. Be the first person in the office, the last one to leave.
2. Be a seeker of knowledge and improve with each day.
3. Do the little things, treat the support staff with the utmost respect.
4. Do the dirty work. Do things that other people don't want to do. Clean up the office, pick up trash, monitor the check in or for curfew. Things of that nature will earn you respect.
5. Listen. Sometimes the less you talk, the more knowledge you can obtain. It is tempting to add your voice to the mix and prove that your way is correct. However, you'll be surprised at what you can learn when you keep your mouth shut.

Don't:

1. Don't act as though you know everything to impress others. The pursuit of knowledge and excellence starts by learning something new.

DO'S AND DON'TS FOR COACHES

2. Don't be late. Being punctual shows that you have respect for others and their time.
3. Don't make promises you can't keep.
4. Don't be the guy that falls asleep in meetings.

About the Author

Jabbar Juluke, a revered figure in the coaching world, brings an impressive journey from a high school head coach to the pinnacle of college football. His path serves as a testament to unwavering dedication and a ceaseless thirst for knowledge. As the Associate Head Coach for a prominent Power 5 school, Juluke has earned his place among coaching elites, and his new book, "Finding & Growing Your Field," is a beacon of inspiration for aspiring coaches and leaders alike.

Juluke's coaching odyssey began in the heart of New Orleans, where he helmed Edna Karr High School to a perfect 14-0 record and a Class 4A state title in 2012. His coaching prowess not only resulted in seven district titles but also paved the way for over 100 of his players to secure college football scholarships at Edna Karr. This early success was a testament to his innate ability to nurture talent and mold young men into upstanding members of their communities.

Before his high school coaching tenure, Juluke embarked on a coaching journey that took him from the defensive coordinator role at Frederick Douglas High School to stints at various high schools, including

ABOUT THE AUTHOR

St. Augustine, Brother Martin and O.P. Walker. This extensive experience at the grassroots level laid the foundation for his future successes in the college ranks.

Juluke's impact transcends the football field. His book, "Finding & Growing Your Field," is a compelling guide to coaching, leadership, and mentorship. It emphasizes the values that define great coaches - respect, integrity, and discipline - values that extend beyond the game and into molding the next generation of leaders. Off the field, Juluke is a devoted family man. He cherishes moments spent with his wife, Denise, and their three children - Jahmad, Jamari, and Dyrius Smith. He enjoys exploring new destinations, savoring diverse cuisines, and experiencing the world with an open heart and an insatiable curiosity.

In "Finding & Growing Your Field," Jabbar Juluke extends an invitation to aspiring coaches and leaders to join him on a transformative journey. He reminds us that coaching is not just about wins and losses, but about leaving an indelible legacy of leadership, respect, and success. Whether you're a young, aspiring coach or a seasoned veteran, Juluke's book is your roadmap to realizing your coaching dreams and making a lasting impact on the lives of those you lead. Join Jabbar Juluke on this remarkable expedition and discover the profound influence you can have on the next generation.

Thank You!

Thank you for embarking on this literary journey with me. Your support means the world. I hope the pages of this book have brought you joy, enlightenment, and inspiration. As you close this chapter, may you carry its wisdom with you and share it with a friend, for knowledge is best when passed on.

JABBAR JULUKE

book FOR speaking

Coach + Educator + Author + Speaker

To book email us at hello@TheEightEighteen.com

TheEightEighteen.com

Made in the USA
Columbia, SC
17 December 2024